New Improved
Limericks

New Improved
Limericks

by
Ernest Henry

Drawings by DAVIZ

Published in Great Britain in 2002
Talking Pig
PO Box 29769, London NW3 3ZU

First published in 1997
Copyright © Text Ernest Henry 1997
Copyright © Illustrations Paul Daviz 1997

ISBN 1 903 520 02 9

Printed in Great Britain by
Turnergraphic Limited

Dedicated to Limerickers
Everywhere.

What's Where,
Where's What,
That's What

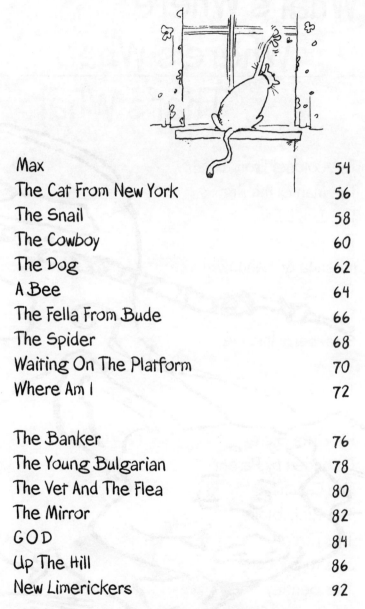

The Colonel From Blighty

There was a colonel from Blighty

Who went to war in his nightie.

The enemy fled

When he got into bed

And refused to return to the fighty.

The Man & His Pig

The man took his pig for a walk
In the park - just he and his pork.
"Let's feed the duck's crackling,
To quieten their cackling,"
Said the pig - who could obviously talk!

The Boy's Ear

The doctor looked in the boy's ear

Which was blocked, so he just couldn't hear.

"The diagnosis is simple:

Remove this 'ere pimple

And you'll have a view distant and clear!"

The Mexican

The Mexican used his machete

To eat a plate of spaghetti.

He couldn't quite masta

The long stringy pasta

And said "The spaghetti? Forgetti!"

Miranda & Manda & Jane

Miranda and Manda and Jane

Had tea in the pouring rain.

Miranda's meringue's

Melted in Manda's hands,

And Jane took a plane off to Spain.

The Rabbit

"Can you imagine," said the Rabbit,

"Giving up my holy digging habit.

Just tell me what is dawn for

If it's not to dig a lawn. For

That's my life - it's what I'm born for, so I'll grab it!"

21

The Actor

The actor *began* to rehearse

Whilst driving his car in reverse.

The problem with that was

His words came out backwards

And some even came out in verse!

OTAROH LLEW M...

Strawberry Jam Pie

Whilst eating a strawberry jam pie,

A fly flew into my eye.

It said "I'm busy inspectin'

The state of the pectin

Which I've done, so I'm off now, bye-bye!"

The Ant

The Ant climbed out of the salad

And started to play a sad ballad.

He sang in A minor

To the startled diner

Who choked on a nice piece of mallard.

The Old Bean

There was an Old Bean on his mower

Who was tired that his mower got slower.

So he thought he would get

A high-powered jet

And suck the lawn straight through its blower.

His Little Sister

(A Triple-Rhymmle)

He tried to hit his sister,
Which he didn't 'cause he missed her,
But his blister of a sister took a bat

And thwacked him on his bot,
Which hurt quite a lot
'Cause the bit she hit
was festering where he sat.

As he writhed in pain he cried "I'm going to get you!"

But she mockingly replied "Did I upset you?

"Well that's tough and serves you right.
And next time you pick a fight,
Don't try it 'cause you might
be knocked out flat!"

Grounded by Parent

(Another Triple-Rhymmle - Cor!)

"It's apparent," said the parent

"That you said you were but weren't

In your school despite the rule that you should.

"And what makes the matter worse, sir,

Is the fact that I'm quite sure, sir,

This could be a precursor - which ain't good!

"So you're grounded from Nintendo for a week now -

And I suggest you think quite hard before you

speak now -

"'Cause if you argue, groan

and grumble

Click your fingers, stomp

or stumble

I'll increase the week

to two... oh yes I would!"

The Cucumber
(Yet Another Triple-Rhymmle)

"I cannot remumber,"

Said the six foot cucumber,

"Which salad I'm supposed to attend.

"Do I get diced up,

Chopped up or spiced up,

Or sliced up from end to end?

"Should I go plain, or get dressed?

Turn up in shorts or string vest?

"Perhaps put a kilt on,

Go with some stilton,

Or squeeze in with a sandwichy friend?"

The Rich Bloke

Whilst busily docking his yacht,

The Rich Bloke said "Look what I've got!

I've earned every bean

Since I was a teen."

...He lied - Mumsy left him the lot!

The Throat

The Doc looked straight down the lad's throat

And exclaimed "My God - there's a boat!

The stern's tied to your tongue,

The bow's down your lung,

Which is why you can't utter a note!"

Bus to Bicester

I took a bus to Bicester
To see my dear old sister.
As she wasn't there,
I walked to Adare
And got a bloody blister.

The Bentley

There was this old chap in a Bentley,

Who took it wherever he wently.

"You can't rush this motor

Like a Toyota:

You have to drive slowly and gently."

Hunting For Fish

I was hunting for fish in the jungle

When a bee bit me right on me tonguel.

As I yelled out in pain,

A lobster from Maine

Pointed out this improbable bungle.

The Barrister's Briefs

The Barrister's briefs were so short

And prepared in time frantic and fraught,

That the ones from the case he

Took out were all lacey:

He'll now be much longer in Court!

The Earwig

The earwig said "Ere, did you 'ear

What happened 'round 'ere just last year?

The Corn on the Cob

Got a brand new job

Growing his ear from 'ere."

Max

Max faxed the facts on his fax

Straight down the phone line to Mack's.

The fact Max had faxed Mack

And Mack then faxed Max back

Meant Mack faxed the facts back to Max.

The Cat From New York

There was a cool cat from New York

Who'd never been out for a walk.

He'd just sit on his mat 'n

His flat in Manhattan

And Comb his tail - with a fork!

The Snail

"It's clear," said the snail on the wall.

"If my suction pads fail, I will fall.

I'd crack open my shell

And feel quite unwell –

So I'd better keep slurping - that's all."

The Cowboy

The cowboy, with hairs on his chest,

Went off to the West in his vest.

When he reached Slough,

He said "That's enough now.

I think I'll stay here for a rest."

The Dog

The dog wondered dozily why
The cat had to worry the fly.
"He could happily gnaw on
This bone with my paw on -
That is if he wanted to die!"

A Bee

A bee is simply a bee

Who buzzes from flower to tree.

If he can't find a blossom,

He'll get angry and toss'em,

And buzz around you and me.

The Fella From Bude

There was a young fella from Bude

Who went off to work in the nude.

He switched on his PC

Which said "Don't let me see

You naked - it's terribly rude!"

The Spider

The spider came right up the spout,

Having caught a fourteen pound trout.

"I'll have it for dinner,"

Said the old silky spinner.

And he did so – and then went back out.

Waiting On The Platform

I've been waiting on the platform for a year

For the train from there to here to appear.

Last month I retired,

The ticket expired:

Which might happen to me – I fear!

Where Am I

Was I just in Diss?

Or was it maybe Liss?

We travelled so fast through

The town we just passed through,

Did I miss Liss, or Diss miss?

The Banker

The banker with the large proboscis
Couldn't tell his noughts from his crosses.
So the bank that he lurked in
And said that he worked in
Made quillions of pounds-worth of losses.

The Young Bulgarian

I know this young Bulgarian

Who's decidedly not vegetarian:

He likes to eat meat

Raw - on its feet -

Which is why he's an octogenarian.

The Vet And The Flea

The Vet said **HALLO! WHAT ARE YOU DOING THERE?** to the Flea.

YES-YOU WERE HERE LAST SATURDAY ON THAT CAT THAT WENT THATAWAY

OH yeah said the Flea.

THAT was Me!

The Mirror

The Mirror that hung on the wall

Looked back at the fat little ball.

It made a correction

In his reflection

And made him look handsome and tall.

GOD

When your head's as spongy as cake,

And your heart is about to break,

Try not to despair,

Believe God is there:

He's just sleeping - but soon will awake.

Up The Hill

(A Streamer-Rhemer)

Up the hill they trundled,
Eager pens and paper bundled,
Off to find the piece of mind that holds the key

To what makes the magic mix
Of words and rhymes in limericks:
They wanted to be limerickers, see!

When at last The Letters loomed fiery red,
The Great Voice shook and boomed overhead:

"If I like the tricks

With which you stitch your limericks,

I'll fix

A crafty mix

Of wicks

And bricks

And alphabetic sticks,

And place imaginary ticks

Against your rhymes and rhymmlericks

So you can pick

And kick

A limerick for me!!"

THE
END

THE
END

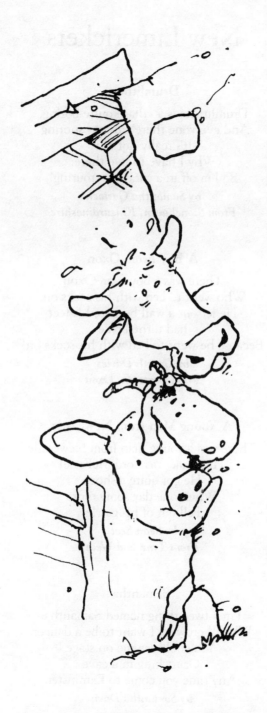

New Limerickers

Drumlithies

Drumlithies is a village quite boring,
And everyone there's always snoring.
It's really not fair
Why I have to live there:
So I'm off in a caravan - touring!
by Samantha Garioch
From Stonehaven, Kincardineshire

A Boy From Oxon

There was a boy from Oxon
Who went to bed with his socks on.
He let out a wail because his feet
had turned pale
Because he went to bed with his socks on!
by Gareth Davies
From Carteton, Oxon

A Young Man from Newcastle

There was a young man from Newcastle
His name was Lord McFassel
He got quite a shock
When one day some rocks
Fell out of his castle.
by Sean Scott
From Tyne and Wear

Samantha

I'm a twee thing named Samantha.
When I grow up I want to be a dancer.
You could see me on stage
Or rocking in a cave
Any time you come to Exminster.
by Samantha Davis
From Exminster

A to Z'ers

Stephanie Selwey from Portsmouth	*A Limerick*
Eleonore Stoddart from Jersey	*Limerick*
Sean Scott from Wallsend	*Newcastle*
Lisette Davis from London	*London*
Rabia Khawaja from Warley	*Smethwick*
Helen Morgan from Broadwell	*Broadwell*
Emma Welsh from West Lothian	*A Girl From Great Britain*
Manjinder Singh from Bradford	*Bradford*
Laura Tisdall from Conkwell	*The Hat*
Laura Crowhurst from Dartford	*Princes Avenue*
Sally Weatherilt from Sale	*The Young Man From Sale*
Lisa Hornberger from Worcester	*Worcester City*
Nadia Alwyn from Worksop	*The Girl From Notts*
Charlotte Noble from Horsham	*The Young Girl From Horsham*

All winners of the A to Z Section of the Fully Booked
National Limerick Competition '97.

Our thanks to **BBC TV's Fully Booked** *for helping us find
these original young limerickers and the A to Z'ers, and we continue our
search for new limerickers in more* **National Limerick Competitions.**

E-mail **your** new limericks to:
limericks@talkingpig.com